Prologue and Acknowledgments

I was born into this world,
To a strong willed young girl.
My mother brought me and raised me, loved
Nurtured, cared for, sheltered and bathed me.
From my first tooth, to my first step,
Always the memories my mother had kept.
She had it hard but rarely she'd show,
that deep inside she'd had been feeling low.
She showed me love and care through my days.
That's why forever, I will preach her praise.
WELL MAYBE AT LEAST I WILL ALWAYS SAY,
THANK YOU DEAR LADY,
WELL I LOVE YOU MOM

To my Wife Theresa and my loves of my life.

Issac and Skye

And special thanks to all the good people who brought me both joyful and painful moments in my life. You are all the reason I survive and push myself and your seasons were all important to me and I am blessed for them.

Thank you dear lord for granting me strength to write down all these processes.

The only Story

If you only remember one thing I say today remember this

Enjoy the time you have, it's the only life your gonna have.

In life we all write a book. Few of us actually put it on paper

The rest just close their book when they pass, they don't pass
it on.

Me I am one of a kind, my book is longer than it should be.

I've lived through way more than someone like me, then

again there is no one like me, I'm the only one left.

Well the only one there has ever been I think, but so are you.

Maybe that's why its hard to understand me. I'm different,

I'm irregular, I'm Special. Things I've heard all my life.

Well things all begin and end with

Page one.

Dan

There once was a man afraid of change.

You might even call this man strange.

But he is only different than you and me

We can only imagine things he has to see.

But why is he scared for another move,

Another life, is he a fool.

What is he happy, or just getting by.

That he must have something, he wont say goodbye.

or does he want to believe, that he can not leave,

Is he scared, or just unprepared.

Worried that he might hurt someone,

Or were there more than one.

He doesn't want to leave,

He just want to relieve,

The stress in his mind, his heart and his soul.

But someday he'll be satisfied,

Someday he will be whole.

He's nothing, but everything all at the same time.

But you'll never know him, his name we shall define.

Dan is his first, and of more you shall thirst,

Sorry but that's all said.

nobody knows if he's alive or he's dead.

But just one more line, the last one from his head.

I give my heart, from the start, love I give all.

For that is my purpose for that was the call.

CLICK..

Inside my head part 15

Some know what I was, so they wont,

Some love me and some don't.

But forever my heart will be full of thoughts,

For that will be all that it will have got.

Love those who love you, and those who don't as well,

For those who hate you Don't say go to hell.

Be caring and daring be one of a kind,

For you alone know what's in your mind,

So remember I'd leave you but never behind.

I'll Love you forever and never at the same time.

For I do not know what the future shall bring,

But like Lennon and Paul wrote a song to sing.

Love is truly all you need,

to help the heart pump the blood your body to feed.

Love always a man,

Who hadn't a plan.

But loved all he touched without his hand.

But he never knew what to do,

So you see he's like you.

You will stay in his heart,

Even if he never met you he'll never forget you

Like a priceless piece of art.

Inside the mind part 10

For all the time I have, I don't have long
And with all the strength I have, I'm not that strong.
For I cant take what I'm given,
It's been like this since the beginning.
So listen to what I say for I'm silent.
Kill me before We become violent.
For though I wouldn't kill, someday you never know,
If this world gets to me, I might finally blow.
Like a volcano erupts, Like the rockets burst,
Like the presidents lies, Make all lives worse.
My mind slowly fades to a darker shade.
Of pale and black, blue and gray.
Multiple colors fill my eyes with sights,
Though mainly dark colors many are bright.
Though things don't seem as good,
As if someone walked to my car and tore of its hood.
And all of the worlds troubles were poured down,
Onto my Motor head and filled the gaps all around.
Bound to carry this weight,
Lord knows I can't wait.
Till this is just a dream,
cause it makes me want to scream.
Want to end this, like taking a piss, allowing shit,
To get off my chest, and yes,
Finally all my mind and body will do is rest.
There are many moments, that show it's, getting better.

Maybe

Maybe I'm crazy

Maybe I'm lazy

Maybe I'm not alright,

Maybe I'm weary

Maybe you cant hear me

Maybe my heads not on too tight

But I feel like I'm not worth a thing.

Until I pick up a mic and begin.

To sing

a song straight from my heart,

That's the start.

To all that is good,

To all that should.

But still through this vail I prevail.

Plan to sail and leave retail.

For a higher calling a better choice,

Something to make all people rejoice.

For with this pen I can extend my voice.

To anyone who must make a choice.

Maybe they are facing the same pain,

Or whether to remain.

Maybe I can

<u>What Love Can Do</u>

Love can break your heart,

Love can tear you down,

It can hurt so bad,

It can toss you round.

It can make you feel so good

And make you happy sometimes.

Love can make you want to sing,

And write down rhymes.

What love can do, Is all up to you.

And what you allow love to do to you.

But Loves Done many a thing to me,

And now the only true thing I see.

What ever love will put you through

Is just a small part of what Love can Do.

She

There She goes isn't She wonderful,

So pretty, gorgeous, Lovely and beautiful.

She's Top of the class, Queen of the hill.

If She does it, everyone will.

She's everything a man could want maybe more

But Oh how I lost my chance years before.

When She was around.

Oh.. when She was Around.

I wasn't seeing quite clear.

I never really saw the awesome, delectable,

Radiant, selectable

Loveable lady near by.

But now I do, my dear I see you.

And In case you care.

To you even She doesn't compare.

And you my love have always been Here.

A Clear Blue Sky

Went to sleep as the rain came down,

My head filled with the thoughts with events past.

The pain and the pleasure, to hate and joy,

I wanted to know how long they would last.

I close my eyes and try to sleep,

But these feelings I have are too deep.

They are so loud though external not a peep.

But at last I fall fast asleep.

The Darkness and pain no longer creep.

The sun comes out over the peeks,

The birds in the trees begin to peep.

I'm ready to wake up to a new Day,

I am so ready to fly.

For all these thoughts are hidden now.

I see a Clear Blue Sky.

I wonder

I wonder where it all went,

how all my hard earned moneys spent

I worked so hard

SO I can party so much.

The party led to pain,

Which led to sleep.

A long time of sleep.

Which hurt my work schedule

Which got me fired,

Which meant no income,

When the rent was Due.

Oh.......

Now I don't worry no more.

Why whats it do

Why is it important, what's it do?

If you prejudge someone else,

They may so judge you.

Accepting each other as people.

Is important in everyway.

So its important to respect, what they are they

do and what they say.

Don't want to battle, Don't want to fight?

Then say the things you know are right.

Respect me and I'll respect you Is how the

saying goes.

So respect others and respect them as friends.

Or they will turn into foes.

I Prefer

I prefer love to hate, I prefer sex to war.

I prefer Moonlight to sunlight.

I prefer Loving myself before loving others.

I prefer school to the streets. I prefer music to picture.

I prefer animals to humans.

I prefer to believe there is more than what is shown.

I prefer friends to foes.

Good relationships to bad acquaintances

I prefer to ask what if and do it than Not do it and dream
what if.

I prefer to find out then believe I'll never know. I prefer
Water to wine.

I prefer being happy with who I am than following others

I'd rather be saddened by the truth than comforted with a
lie.

I prefer to kiss the morning than kissing up.

I prefer talking things out. I prefer a diploma to a GED

I prefer females , I prefer moonlit walks. I prefer to write, I
prefer the blues, But nothing beats rock and roll.

I prefer not to vote, I prefer myself over press.

I prefer to make my own mistakes

I prefer the faith I have to the gossip I hear. I just prefer life.

Working Man

Life ain't easy for a working man,

The ladder grows harder to climb.

Working day in and working day out,

All for a nickel and dime.

What they pay's not worth my time,

But it's the wage received for this crime.

To pay the bills and live my life,

I must give, through the stress and strife.

No mortal man can survive with out a plan,

For we all become the working man.

Women as well find this fate,

All past and present as of late,

Harder sometimes to keep up this pace,

In this never ending rat filled race.

But finding what you love to do,

That makes some money and satisfies you to.

Then a working man shall you be.

But only in title and image you see.

For your having fun, getting paid for your joy.

It is no longer your soul you employ,

But your spirit enthralled, elated and free,

And no longer a working man shall you be.

Fail or Succeed

Live your own way, Die your own way.

Fail or succeed, just do it your own way.

Fail or Succeed, when you feel the need.

To climb over mountains, or just wait and bleed.

Success is only determined, by the goals we set.

So listen now and never forget

Fail or succeed just have no regrets.

Do it for your yourself do it each and every day.

Fail or Succeed, Just do it your way.

A Bloody Mess

A bloody mess remains throughout,

This heart of mine which has been thrown about

A Bloody mess which is unclean,

From hate which has been provoked against me.

A bloody mess which came from many depressing acts of hate,

That hurts so much and leaves me in a love lost state.

Because of this the people I care too much about,

Who now put this pain in my heart.

That don't care enough for a depressed soul.

To give a helping hand to a friend who falls.

That now may act as though you are,

A friend who's friends with them all.

The Heart

The heart last longer than the mind,
You'll still have love from those left behind.
From family and friends to loves of the past.
Though your gone, their love for you lasts.
Memories are saved in the heart,
Your mind just digs them out.
Your souls makes them shine,
But your heart feels what they're about.
The heart gives love that can change nations at war.
Love brings peace and understanding
of what its all for.
May you live with the passion of one who loves all.
And never shall when you stumble shall fall.
But glide on the strings of the Heart that's within.
And never shall one thing end just another begin.

In My Head part 41
I don't know what I'm doing.
Am I going the right way or am I screwing
things up for my future generations,
And my current relations.
Ships floating on the sea of my mind,
Get lost and sail off and get left behind.
Behind me go all my blues,
In this life only enemies lose,
Themselves never me, for I you see,
Flow like Ali with my poetry.
But I'm oh so pretty, yet sting like a bee.
Flowing like a river, never knowing where I bend.
Like a game with no clock my hustle never ends.
I shall not be stopped by another's plans for me.
For only My ideas create my destiny.
My piece of mind, my peace I mind.
My piece of this great American pie.
My freedom to do as my heart says to do.
And know the difference between
what is owed and what is due.
For I only do, what I was sent here to do.
Not chicken to face this world, no Perdue.
So as I complete this short monologue.
And give you a big underdog.
I leave you to swing and control your own fate.
Do not deviate once we separate.

First and goal

Still not satisfied with what I got,
I could have the world, if I had the shot.
I do things others won't,
I have things inside that many don't.
I live my life day to day,
I mean almost every word that I say.
I'm straight forward and rarely do I hold back.
I'm quick with my time, so pick up the slack.
And as I run on first and goal.
I lead with my mind, heart, body and soul.
So if you want to come along hold tight, don't let go
But don't hold be back cause I sure won't slow.
I write what I feel, and always keep it real.
To enjoy my life is my only ordeal.
With the crowd on their feet I cross the threshold.
My name I hear beginning to become bellowed.
But not from the world of exterior perception.
But more of a soulful full body reflection.
That states I have succeeded in pleasing myself.
My heart to my mind, good job it tells.
So I release the tension once more in my hand.
The pad is now full I've written all I can.
I've opened the sealed container within.
And loaded all on this field of paper with my pen.

For yourself

Jumping to your death, you can hear the screams,
So loud that they wake you right up from this dream.
No longer can you hide the truth,
For they are all onto you.
They know the pain you hide.
The hatred deep inside.
The way you close your eyes, and never cry.
You want to go away, but here is where you stay.
Drowning in your own internal river of tears,
Your fears, and thoughts of the world.
That your not enough for your young baby girl.
You don't know where life's leading, your bleeding,
And pleading.
For this life to show you
all of the love you've been needing
But they teach you and preach you are the one who
starts feeding.
Your heart with the love you so treasure.
Loving thyself is the only way to measure.
The love you can offer,
and the world will seen brighter
The burden of stones that you carry will seem lighter.
The path to your greatness and purpose will shine.
The truth and happiness shall be thine.

That's life part 2

I have to sleep away thoughts of pain,
They flow like raindrops on my window Paine.
Like the minutes of my life, wasted youth passed quick.
From work and stress, no shit I'm getting sick.
Of lifes up and downs make me so nauseous,
I have become so scared, thoughtful and precautious.
Wondering who's out to get me, and what will affect me.
But still I must push on and be stay strong.
For my son and my daughter
And any seeds I shall father.
The people that stress me out, though I love, give me hell,
But I guess I'm the devil so it's all just as well.
That I assume blame, and the same old to deal with.
And turn into positive reinforcement.
With reimbursement I give all I can.
I do all I can and all I wants love in demand.
That's life don't you know, face the curtains with a bow.
For life is a show. You're the star any how.
The role may change even superman plays the fool.
Just remember that's life. That's the only rule.

Going to hell

I'm going to hell, leaving this place I call home,
So you can be happy cause with me you feel alone.
So I'm leaving on the fast lane,
Don't know if I'll be back again.
I might be getting hurt by pain, But it will mend with sweet refrain.
Packing my bags on a holiday.
Be gone and you won't have to see me.
Ever again and the child I am
Will play a different game
I'm going to hell
The devils calling my name
Since I only seem to do wrong,
I must disappear.
to the burning pits.
Since theres no more for me here
I will call it quits.

I'm Coming home

I'm coming home, once I'm finished all my work,
Because you know I'll be done soon.
I'm coming home, When the sun starts going down,
I'll be home in the room.
Soon I'll be where I want to be
Home with you, together.
I hope that you feel the same way what so ever.
Forever I will always be,
Truthful to you if your for me.
me and you, you and me,
That is what we'll always be.
I'm coming home, I'll be there soon.
Soon you won't be alone.
Once my job is finished I will be on my way home,
I'm coming home, Finally I'm coming home.

What's love?

What is love, Can you put it in a box,
can you carry it in a bag.
Can you share it with everybody,
can you give it away.
Is it only in one person or everyones' soul.
Does it come from people talking,
Does it come from Rock and roll.
Does it grow bigger by age,
Or get smaller after youth
I know sometimes It's good,
But found that's not always true.
It's bad to think it'll always last,
Cause you'll just end up hurt.
Though many don't know what it is,
We all have a heart
And if love could be put in a box
We each could take our part.
It's easy to fall into it.
But it hurts you when it's done.
So remember there's a lot of love,
So don't feel bad losing some, I'm Done.

Where's my Juliet

I keep hearing that my friends were all in love.
They met their love, like Romeo, by looking up above.
Now why don't you look up to one, is what they say
It's about time I try, I guess I'll start today.
I look up but like I thought before,
There was nobody there, what did I look for.
Where is my Juliet, my angel from above.
I think I've found one, I think I've found a love.
My friends are now all single looking at me.
Asking me, how lucky a guy I must be?
To have a love this faithful, to have a love this true.
We need some help with love, tell us what to do.
Up there is no Juliet, no angel from above.
Just look around my friends, there is plenty of love.
To the one I found, my Juliet, I your Romeo.
Can't wait to see how far this will go.

A New Life

A new life, born again, another time around.

A way to make up for everything I did wrong.

More time to right this wrong, time for one more song

To leave and die in peace.

Time to say the things I never said.

That I wanted to say but didn't take the time.

To be alive again, To be a man again.

To be a friend, a lover, a child

A son of sons

To let go of the past and be one.

My one to be true.

A whole new life.

I must live without you.

Welcome to my world

Welcome to my world,
Now you see what I see.
What do you think?
Do you feel you can walk,
Even a mile in my shoes.
Do you like my life?
Would you like to live it.
Would you want to be me?
Are you sick of being you.
I'm not sick of being me.
In fact I'm fine.
Welcome to my world,
A world that is all mine.

I took the fall

Carry me, for I can't walk.

Read my lips, For I can't talk.

I lost all I had, Lost it all.

I lost my world, when I took the fall.

I should have listened, and not have ran.

Into the fire and took my stand.

Should have kept on going,

But I thought I had no chance.

I thought I couldn't go on, had nobody who cared.

But now I know I can, now that you're here.

I took the fall, But I didn't lose it all.

I still got you,

that's all I need cause I love you.

Just another escape

Getting out of this hole,
My words have one escape.
Through this pencil I speak, and life un-complicates.
Life becomes so clear but for just a short moment,
Though this is my mind, I do not own it.
The thoughts are wild,
The inner workings of a child.
That grew up so fast that it must reconcile.
With the being becoming, the outer flesh it consumes,
To give the inner soul its ample room.
To groom, and illuminate,
the conjugated words the being can't understand.
So the spirit can take control of his little hands.
Until every thought is released and performed.
To alleviate the tension and leave the soul warm.
Inside the carcass of this thirty year old child,
Who has been for 10 or 20 so wild.
Now through the eyes of his own child.
Sees the youth he once had and stays glad in his heart.
His soul is at rest now his body can start.
To unwind from the time he spent in this race.
At too quick and absurd a reckless pace.
The pencil now leadless all words did withdraw,
From the mind and soul through this tool like a straw
Just another escape from the madness he saw,
Now this child can stare at the souls thoughts in aw..

Just one more year

Just one more year, Till the plan disappears,
And I'm left contemplating where I go from here.
Do I stretch five more in, Do I throw old dreams out.
Should I live with some demons, or flush them all out.
Could I with my demons, live happy with no doubt,
Or would life be simpler If I lived without.
Do I start a rumble in my lifes painful foundation.
Or leave all alone and live with this temptation.
That chip in my shoulder should as flaws I see.
Certain issues it takes charge while others it flees.
Wish I could control it, turn it on and off.
I fear with change what I have will be lost.
Though surely it has come to a halt and undoing.
This state parts of me are in
with my life they are screwing
When will I be free you may ask me my dear.
The path to me is not quite clear.
But my answer to all
Just one more year.

Signs of life (the saga)
Family

It seems all the god times are overshadowed by the bad
But still I feel blessed to have,
Had the moments I have had.
I know I had a father but my mother carried on.
Shes the strongest person I know.
Know so many people who had less stress and were gone.
That's why my family is tough and will never die,
Though we have had it rough, we won't say goodbye.
We all need family to stay strong forever more,
As fish need water to swim and birds air to soar.
The strength of family is one that is sure and pure.

Friendship

We met on a bad note,
But it ended up well.
I was having a bad day and you surely could tell.
We started to talk one thing begins as another ends.
Then we became the closest of friends.
This friendships getting so strong,
All this trust is forever long,
Belonging to you, because your real,
And know you always know the way that I feel.

Love
Love; It concurs every heart.
Love; It could break us apart.
When I see you I feel love,
Whether I'm feeling sad and love or happy and lively,
You make my day shine even more brightly.
Like walking on the clouds above the earth below.
I hope this feeling will forever grow.
And we would try to make this last,
Till the future becomes the past,
Till all lives have passed.
I will love you always.
Through all of my nights and all of your days.

Sorrow
This isn't working out, this is not what I want.
I wanted someone who I could talk with,
Walk, and live and go to war with.
That's not what we have so push come to shove.
We gat to have it all, we must have love.
So since we don't we are through.
Sorrow sinks in me, and I feel sorry for you.

Hate

I hate you, I never want to see you again.
Get away from me, Leave me alone.
I don't like you at all, I wish you would die.
I wish you weren't here, I wish you were gone.
So forget everything I ever promised you.
None of it will ever come true.
Our love died and is buried forever.
I hate you, Don't come back. Ever.

Regret

Why did I say those hurtful things,
Why did I act that way.
Why did I ever put you down,
Why'd I ever run away.
Why did I end everything we had,
Why did I stop all the love.
Why didn't we talk before,
The pushing turned into shove.
I need to make amends,
I need us to be friends again.

Forgiveness

I want to apologize for anything I put you through,
For any pain I Never meant for you.
How we were both at fault for why we split,
I realize we should be friends and all this trouble forget
Forgiveness is all we need to give it another try.
So let's figure out what we were before we said goodbye.

Lovers

Through our pain and pleasure,
When we began to our times apart.
Forever my lover, your forever in my heart.
I love when were together,
I cry when we must part.
I'm glad we gave this affair,
A chance for a second start.

Why get married

Why get married you already have my life.
We don't need the agreements for you to be my wife.
I'll give you a ring, If you really need one.
But if you want a wedding, I'll get it done.
We'll get a priest, a church, a tux and a dress,
If that's too much, a courthouse or have less.
I'll love you, till death do us part.
But why get married when you already own my heart.

The Cycle Continues

A new life begins when a child is born,
Gaps between family and friends are all worn.
Now we begin the Cycle again,
Like we Did way back when.
When we were born and our parents before,
Cause this is what all should live for.
To continue the chain in this everlasting circle of life,
Through the painful, joyful, strainful years we survive.
To let the cycle continue in this world evermore.
As the cycle continues........

Inside my head part 15
I'm a man, not a boy anymore.
I've already learned so much more.
Then possibly I should have by my age.
But strange are the stages of life these days.
I've learned about love, respect and joy.
I've learned at a young age that it isn't a toy.
But I've mainly learned that life isn't easy,
Actually it is quite tough.
It isn't promised to all, you must have the right stuff,
I have so much to say,
But I've said quite enough.

Inside my head Part 16 (being bored)
Feel light headed, about to faint,
Don't really want to sleep,
For creepy thoughts and visions
Into my head do creep.
Things that happen to me when the lights go out.
Things that being bored,
Always bring about.
Make me believe sleep I can do without.

Crazy

I don't know what to do with life,
Thought by now it would all be done,
I'm still alive? Kind of sort of.
I'm in Pennsyltucky working at Wally.
Still Happiness is far from being complete.
I live on these moments.
I cling to those moments.
I live my life for those moments.
Maybe I'm Crazy.
But all the greats say
you gotta keep that little crazy.
Well I've kept too much.
I live on it.
Day by day a little more
Sneaks in more and more.
Do don't listen to the clever lines I say.
I'm Crazy. Heee heee heee.

Happy

Do you think I'm really this happy,
This well off this sappy
Think I enjoy every breath I take,
Well that part is true
That part will always be, I do
Enjoy my breaths and you should too.
Life is a gift, not everyone can enjoy it,
Some die early, some never try to see
That life is a one time gig, Live it happy.

Hopeless

Day by day
Sorrow fills my heart,
Hopeless desires are all that I have got.
Temptations bring on crossroads
Of which I must choose a path.
For if I choose the right road,
It shall lead me back.
From this hopeless part of life,
To a fulfillment of my dreams,
So life could be much different,
And better than it often seems.

Look

People look with their eyes,
Instead of their hearts.
And see only what they want.
What's on the outside.
Cause if they could look with their hearts,
Instead of their eyes.
They could see inside.
Then they would understand who I am.
And no more would we hide.

What's going on

Whats going on it the world today
People wake up and get killed each day.
Don't believe it would happen to you,
What do you think,
DO you think they knew.
Didn't get to say their final goodbye,
Didn't kiss their kids so they wouldn't cry.
All this time wasted without showing care,
What's going on?
Does anyone care.
Whats going on?
Is this what the human race has decided on,
Whats going on?
Do we kill each other to find out.
What's going on?
Is there any choice.
Whats going on?
In this world full of doubt.
What's going to be left in this world.
What about little boys and little girls.
Why do we have to bring on tears and cry.
Why do so many people have to die.
What's going on?
I see it and fear.
That one day I too may well disappear.
So I spend every second I can with those that are dear.
Showing them my love, respect and care.

Fools heart

Look at that guy,
That well brought up young man.
Living as if the world revolves around him.
That guy in his suit has a fools heart.
He'd fall for anything.
See there's a new red sports car.
There's another gold watch.
There another big chain around his neck.
Like a noose around a hung witch in Salem.
That is not it as you see.
That well brought up man.
Is a gambler you see.
And I think he's out of luck.
And with one wrong toss of the dice.
His life could really be ....

Save it for the next
All your lies, All your tears
All the pain through the years.
All the cheating,
All the heartbreak,
all the time.
All the love we could have had.
Anytime that we got mad.
You can take all I have.
In text and in mind.
And save it for the next man in line.

Rock Hard
Where I slept the pillows are rock hard.
The blankets get colder during the night.
You can hear the traffic and wind blow,
You can feel the tension oozing through
Your body like melted butter on crusty toast.
You know what it is to have a bad night.
But you don't need much to stay there.
Just the strength to survive,
Through the rain, sleet hail and snow.
So sleep tight in your bed.
With a pillow beneath your head.
And I'll get back on the road.
Goodnight!

The Unwanted Heart
The heart that is all for love,
And not for looks alone.
That's the heart that no one has,
A heart that's mine alone.
An unwanted man has an unwanted heart.
But the unwanted man has a lot to hide,
He must hide the unwanted heart inside.

The knife in my heart
The nife in my heart still gives me pain,
But to the public my tears I contain.
For I've lost again, my heart is in pain.
For the knife Love has left still remains.
And has me singing the same refrain.
The same.
Something no one takes out by showing love.
But I'll survive since I'm still strong enough.

Friends

Friends are with you through thick and thin,
They love you when you lose not just when you win.
They put up with you in good times,
And help you during bad.
They"ll always be with you, for you.
Even if you make them mad.
They will love you forever, even after you die,
They know when you are truthful and when you tell a lie.
They are as close as family, close knit, they fit,
That's what a friend is,
And that's all I got to say about it.

I'm not far behind

I keep trying and trying
But still you don't see.
Why I care and how much you mean to me.
You're a great friend and I hope it stays that way,
Stay in touch, keep strong come what may.
So take care of yourself,
And keep me in mind.
If your ever in need of comfort,
I'm not far behind.

Good

It's over. Good. So I can take my heart back.

After giving you my life and getting none back.

After giving you things you needed and what you want,

I can finally stop crying for what I haven't got.

I can. Good.

I have been waiting to.

It's over. Good. I'm over you.

I didn't want to have a love who didn't care.

All I wanted was a soul with a love to share.

So Adios, Bye bye see you later.

Not. I will find a better lover.

It's over. Good.

I'm glad it's over.

Its finally over.

The streets
In the streets where I lived,
There are people dying.
But what can I do to change it. NOTHING.
I wish I could do more But I can't.
Too Bad.
The streets and the people must die.
Like bugs to god, to heave they shall go.
Luck can't help them, nothing can.
Too bad.
What can one man do but see.
The streets where I lived are dark.
They are full of pain, but I cant change it.
Too bad.
All I can do is speak of it,
Spread the word and care.
But is that really enough.
Its more than other do.
But its not enough,
It wasn't enough.
The streets have gone cold.
No pumping, no streaming.
Just still and quite.
Too. Bad.

The lonely

The lonely people have fun,
Even though they are alone,
Even though they are on their own.
Even though people put them down.
When they walk on the streets of town.
The lonely people are the best people to know,
They know things others don't,
Though the popular kids let you down,
The lonely people won't.
The lonely people have fun.
They live all for one.
They work hard and play it cool.
There are no lonely people who are fools.
SO next time you see,
A lonely girl or boy.
Stay close to see.
Them fill your life with joy.
Soon you will understand,
The world of this
Gentle man.

Pain and Pleasure

What is the difference between pain and pleasure

One we live with, the other we treasure.

We savor the pleasure, like a new York strip.

Then the pain comes and makes you abandon ship.

Pain is pain, its as natural as rain.

Pleasure is Pleasure, not enough we complain.

Pleasure is pain when it's your heart someone is playing.

Hurting your soul with the things they are saying.

From flirting with others, when your supposed to be lovers.

To fooling around between the covers.

Who knows which is pain and which is pleasure,

When it comes to love it is strange.

That the most pleasuring moment is also the most painful
exchange.

Losers in Paradise

We walk around, thinking about what can be,
If we'll be here tomorrow, perhaps not we'll see.
Dreaming of good times, singing in the morning sun,
The games we played , the things we've won.
The girls we knew, the boys as well.
The people we like and one we told go to hell.
We're just losers in paradise.
Dreamers on the street.
Things we have, and people who we meet.
Are all part of a losers paradise.
Cause we're just losers who win in paradise.
I hope that's how it'll be.
We'll be winners in paradise.
It could happen you'll see.
Fore now losers in paradise we still must be.

Cold and lonely

It's cold and lonely,

Out here on the streets.

Walking around with no shoes on my feet.

The alcohol wore off

I wandered the streets till the end.

I'm broke and tired and in need of a friend.

Can you help this poor old man.

By giving me some money or giving me a hand.

It's hard when your on your own.

It's hard when it's lonely.

To be cold and to be following the only,

Person you can when there's nobody there.

Goodbye for now, for you can come back again.

But hopefully for me this isn't the end.

I Don't want to go away pt 2

Don't do me any favors for your attitude has said enough.

I guess these last few years have meant nill,

meant nothing so forget it.

Three years of my life, three summers here, seems like that meant spit.

Go home enjoy your night,

Thanks for the check.

Too bad its Saturday night, and money is tight.

I guess you could see.

Nor did you know I only had two hours of sleep.

But still had the respectful want and love to come.

To play for you, to come and perform some.

I don't want to go away but when my hours,

Are adding up,

Yet my pay is going down.

You feel I owe you my soul for giving me a platform.

So I must be your monkey and perform.

For what ever rotten bananas you have in your bag.

Well tonight it ends, as the last dancer bends.

I will not longer be your steady teddy,

Bringing you joy, when you needed and barely getting a nudge when love is due in return.

I don't want to go, but here we go, as the last vocals blow.

I leave you with this refrain.

Listen to the music, and in a song you love I'll return again.

I am the only one

The only one, knows the ways of my life can change .

I am the only one whos lifestyle is strange.

The only one with a messed up family,

Messed up legs I have too.

The few things left though many are few.

They consist of music, pen, pad and you.

My heart, my soul inside me are strong.

But I am the only one my mind drags along.

For this roller coaster of a life with is head spinning turns.

I am the only one for whom my spirit yearns.

It yearns to be with me alone.

To dissolve those dark images into bright colored hues.

To show me where I am going and which paths to choose.

Since at times I am the only one on this road.

My spirit

Maybe not but I take all good things coming my way.
Cause not many good things are left today.
Maybe the plan is to take my hand,
and finish what was started.
Help the hurt, Cause I'm kind hearted.
Give respect to those departed, But still theirs pain,
For only I can change the rain,
Into a river of words, that flows through your ears,
To relieve the stress and wash away hurt of the years.
The only one, the loaded gun, the sinners son, for everyone,
I'm here, I care, I live, I give, I listen and learn.
I feel, I heal, I help let it burn.
For through my mother I learned to love others.
And though my father left pain,
I love like no other and always remain the same.
Playing my games to enjoy life,
Pass through this struggle and strife.
For I've let you inside,
No I have nothing to hide.
The unknown poet is known to some,
If you feel you can be healed, I want you to come.
Listen in for your turn, Listen in maybe even learn.
That I alone condone your soul, for I have control of the key
For the heart to see,
What is left inside, love life, and you'll strive,
And finally be the one to drive.
Your heart to that wonderful place of joy.
Enjoy each step weather you're a girl or boy.
Always be open for more, for a closed door,
Leaves your soul sore.
But open skies allow your spirits to soar.
Bon Jure.
Love always the unknown poet...

Let me escape pt 1

Let me run away, frolic and play,

I let everyone else, What do you say?

It's no longer June, nor is it May,

What you might think, could be the right way,

So let me escape, let me do it today.

Let me escape pt. 2

Good morning! Still here.

Thought you got loose, I was unaware.

That you are physically tied to this chair.

As if in a cage without rage full of fear.

Come to me and don't be scared.

Help me escape and we'll both make it there

Let me escape pt. 3

I'm breaking free ha ha he hee

I'm a break free, no shackles on me.

No formal address, no identity,

Though everyone still seems to think they know me.

Do you know me? Am I what you think?

Do you understand, are you a shrink.

For If you are not, you don't know the plot

I am free from these chains that you brought.

Feelings

Feelings run through my body

like a train running through town

I like the trains but sometimes the train

doesn't stay long enough.

I wish I could tell the conductor, to stop and wait.

But he never listens nobody listens.

They are all the same,

Human

What makes these feelings come and go

Is it god, is he that great conductor who doesn't listen

Or is it the dead people. Have they found a way into your head and like to say to you how do you like it.

This is what they did to us.

No its just in your mind.

You people think too much.

Feelings are things your mind and heart send

Throughout your body, yeah.

That's my train coming in, I guess I got to go,

I'll see you later though, maybe.

Remember me (a song)

V1: no one could ever take your place.

Though its been years since I saw your face.

Before you went to the lord above.

You spent your days showing me nothing but love.

You were closer to me than my own dad.

You were like the father I was should've had.

Chorus: We wish you will hear our prayers,

We all miss you way down here.

All I want you from you, you see,

Is for you to remember me.

V2: We are now lost and troubled severely,

So I'm sending you our love sincerely.

Grampa you were always there for me,

All I have to ask is for you to remember me

Remember me in heaven tonight,

Don't worry for us we'll be alright

(repeat chorus)

Inside my head verse 6

I wish for times where I have no time,

No work, no trouble, nothing, no hustle.

Me time, where I can start thinking of me,

No thoughts of anyone else,

Forget everyone else for a while and just think of my self.

Not he, or she, or it or her or him or them or they,

Or can't or wont or will or don't or perhaps or maybe, may.

Or tensions, attentions, detention, perfection, pretention,

Just me and what I can do to better my situation, and such

But I believe I think too much, maybe that is my problem,

No I have no problem. I just think I do,

I should take a break from these things life puts me through

These are just thoughts right, they are all in the mind,

Thoughts that should all be kept or left far behind.

So let me try to shelf these thoughts,

But sometimes thoughts are all I got.

All I have left is my mind all though it is half gone.

But again these are just thoughts behind a door,

Thoughts that's all folks, but stay tuned there's more.